Kaleidoscope

Milagros Diaz

ISBN 978-1-63784-299-7 (paperback)
ISBN 978-1-63784-300-0 (digital)

Copyright © 2024 by Milagros Diaz

All rights reserved. No part of this publication may be reproduced, distributed, or transmitted in any form or by any means, including photocopying, recording, or other electronic or mechanical methods without the prior written permission of the publisher. For permission requests, solicit the publisher via the address below.

Hawes & Jenkins Publishing
16427 N Scottsdale Road Suite 410
Scottsdale, AZ 85254
www.hawesjenkins.com

Printed in the United States of America

Creations

As I look at the crystal blue waters, my body becomes possessed.
Observing the beauty through my eyes as it passes through my visual being, onto my mental being.
Much as the creatures swim in the depth of the sea, so do the words in the depth of my mind.
These words flow from the mind through my arms and onto my hands; like the waters into streams far in a distance.
My alter ego takes control from then on and gives birth to words of emotion onto a pure whiteness; allowing the ink to materialize beautiful verses.
Something composed as naturally as the crystal blue waters.

Sudden Warning

The clouds cheerless and dreary
The wind blowing heavily and unannounced
Squalling through the streets and sky.
The day has unexpectedly turned dark as the ground below
Before you know it, the rain will soon pour down
Upon our pavements and bodies
And soak through like a cleansing
Bath that has long been awaited.

A cascading downpour that will clear out
Our tension and wash away our silent tears.
The rain has fallen and ceased, the sun's shadow seeping
Allowing a faint formation of a rainbow.

What happened to the rainfall?
Where did the unanticipated cloudburst go?
A quiet and immediate shower that came and went without warning.
A short period of time that made us realize
Not to forget that our Father above, is still in existence.

Hope and Faith of a better tomorrow will never die!

Say Cheese!

An awkward smile trapped inside a glass frame
The camera doesn't lie, but it does tell a story.
A black shiny gown draped over me accompanied by a tilted hat, with a flat top
To show the world all I have accomplished.
The smile is fake and my heart damn near silently still.
The picture shows a smiling face
With an invisible tear swaying down the curves of my cheeks.
Undetected. Unnoticeable. Unapologetic.

Nobody sees the pain and sorrow that I'm going through
My picture, a photo capturing a symbol of success.
A time of glory, a time to shine
But the flash is out and the spark withdrawn.
Yet there I stand alone. All smiles and applause for me and all to see.

A former self trapped. Catering to the expectations of others. Unaware. Unbeknownst. Uninvited.

Don't forget to smile!

Say cheese!

Frightening Call

Strolling down the beach
I stared deep into the profound blue sky
The ocean waves splashing against the jetty
And all of a sudden I wanted to cry.
My heart cradled in silence for not one tear would fall
Admiring the clouds, gazing at the wild blue yonder as if that someone would call.

I needed to hear a call…

A call from the beyond
A call that no else would hear, but me
But as I stood there—WAITING—I felt a sudden fear.
Swiftly regained focus and thought to myself:
You're searching for a call that is not yet for you to hear.

So I continue to dawdle and ramble with my shadow at my heels following so tall
And mumbled to myself:
Will I hear a call? Am I ready to be called upon?

Nightmare in Disguise

Goggled at myself in the mirror and mumbled, "This is it!"
Inhaled a deep breath and walked down the stairs
Beautifully dressed and emotions invisibly in hysterics,
I observed the colored faces assembled in their seats
Suddenly, the chord of the piano struck and so did my nerves
Apprehensively, I stood behind the audience, as I smelled the wax of
    candles burning
The flickering of lights fidgeting, and the aroma of incense and flow-
    ers surrounding the room.

>   Then an internal voice uttered:
>   "Who picked these flowers?"
>   "Where are the familiar faces?"
>   "Where is my happiness?"

Legs trembled under my elegant gown, escorted by unwelcomed déjà
    vu sentiments
Suspicious of all emotions and overwhelmed of being in the presence
    of my significant other,
I was panic-stricken, jailed by foul thoughts from empty promises.
A slight faintness bestowed upon me and I surveilled the surrounding
    judgments.
With my Savior positioned on the Cross above me,
A man of cloth fashioned to enact his blessed duties beside me,
I stood before this camouflaged man, his spiked tail neatly tucked
    away
My future, my damnation.
Can I hold on much longer?

The fear of letting everyone down.
Can I just walk away?
Yes, I must because "to death do us part"
Is an incarcerated contract with no escape!

I'm sorry, I never meant to hurt you!

Lost Love

The joyous marching band that harmonized in my heart did nothing to dispel your dejection
Self-forced to renounce love due to previous scars not yet healed, convicted him with a desolate heart
Hoarded memories blighted any *new love—my love.*

Drunken words of yesterday recorded in my mind, inflicted with false hope
Lost to grief, knowing that once you were somebody's option, but now nobody's choice
Apathetic to any *new love—my love.*

Love isn't a game of X's and O's for to play the game, willing participants have to partake
Time to delve and reset. Roll the dice, hit a bullseye, and pin the tail on a new love
Time waits for no one and no one has the time to lose
Whimsical as love can be, take a chance not with *any love—my love.*

Consummate

Random kisses, playful hugs, and intense emotions
That's how our love commenced.
An invited gesture overwhelmed our bodies
And our heartbeats harmonized as one.
The initial pain indicated the union of our souls
For departure was unknown.
Our eyes met and unheard words were spoken
Heard by the silence that filled the air
With uncontrollable love and ignited flare.
Clutched hands, steamy breath, drinking in the beauty of "Amor"
In mute agreement, we'll reach the highest point of ecstasy
And find our climax.

Babies

Babies…

Aborted, abandoned, adopted, unloved
A Miracle from God
Created to suffer if not born.

Left in dumpsters, doorsteps, orphanages, streets
Created from mistakes, passions, rapes, ignorance.

Innocent, naïve, soft, cuddly
Conceived and delivered without regard.
Yet the cause of numerous conundrums
Created by

Adults…

Babies…

Doubt

Never did you give me reason to doubt
Yet I can't help but wonder.
Never once did you reveal a clue
That there may be another love down yonder.
My insecurities were very well in place
Though I wrestled and wavered the love you had for me.
The anxieties in my heart are all at a race
Because for me, you're my only cure and remedy.
Your love has always been true
So never should I doubt it.
Our worlds combined has set my life anew
And it's as angelic as the Heavens above.
Keeping in my mind always, the capabilities that love can endure
Not allowing to be fooled and bewildered with unnecessary doubt.

Sealed with a Kiss

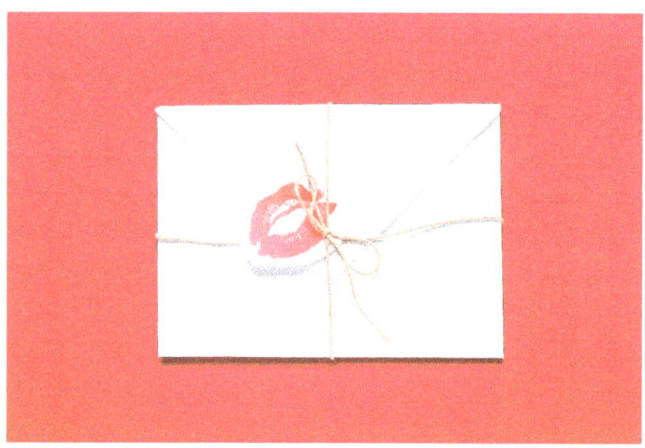

There's so much of your love I miss
Though you may not have the imagination to know.
Yet every night I sit and write you letters
And seal them with a kiss.
I study your face carefully in my mind
And keep it locked away
For you are my one and only love
Which I tend to someday again find.
Searching high and low for the love I desire, but disappeared.
Still I can't get you out of my heart,
The man I love from head to toe.
Waiting for you, I look out the window
My heart is not at bliss.
So I will continuously write you letters
Sealed with a Kiss!

Let Me Not, But Let Me

Let me not think of the places I'm going, but the places I've been.
Let me not forget of difficult obstacles, misfortunes, and regrets.
Let me not fail to recall all the "could of," "should of," and "would ofs" in my life.
Let me not bury the memories, thoughts, or contemplations that led me to a monochrome state.
Let me not be terror-stricken of embracing the iridescent light that is due to thy self.
BUT…
Let me envision new venues, pleasant journeys, and unpack the compass to a new existence.
Let me get accustomed to marching untraveled steps, and unchartered waters.
Let me construct fond memories of precious moments, with the ability to claim its spirit.
Let me remember to collect souvenirs throughout my journey without feeling the silhouette of my past.
Let me connect my heart, body, and soul and abandon the stigma once stamped on my life's passport.

Vulnerable

I've allowed myself to be vulnerable to his touch. Let my defenses down and open a gateway of affection and undisguised emotion.

To be opportunistic and bask in his embrace while battling the urge to connect with his kiss.

My predilection for his heart was undoubtedly noticeable. Uncertain of his feelings, I've taken the chance to be brave and risk the unknown.

My heart, an undisclosed location to so many beforehand. A mere dreamscape where one's fantasy was untouched and protected from all offense.

In accordance with my heart, no need to rue this decision. I've allowed myself to be susceptible to love and all that it encompasses.

My heart's blueprint visible to the naked eye yet at arm's length. However, his body called me with a soft whisper. I've weakened and granted access.

Traffic

The sea of red lights was an indication of what lay ahead.

A feigned smile appeared on my lips, thoughts running a mock thinking of this clandestine affair formed from a simple handshake and a soft grin.

It was in my best interest to make a U-turn, step on the gas, and continue forward without looking back.

Unapologetically I pumped my brakes and allowed a new passenger. All warning signs flooded my mind.

Signal to stop and eject this unplanned traveler.

Yield and halt the feeling of these salacious ideas of me and him.

Do not enter for there is no available entry.

No more room for another broken heart. My beating muscle has been smashed so many times before. Bits of fragments recollected and replaced, like a puzzle. The strength that it takes to clear roadblocks after a crash, takes a toll on my soul.

His tender touch interrupts my daydreaming. The unhurried traffic dispersed, and our lips accelerate with confessions of love for one another.

Our words are hazardous. No operating manual to guide this traffic jam of emotions. Time for one of us to get off this ride and hitchhike on another road.

Some pavements are destined to be traveled alone and others accompanied.

Follow the speed limit.

Avoid any wrong ways, and

Stay clear of dead ends.

Love is a two-way street, where we all cross paths and jaywalk to our final destination.

A Rued Moment

One Sunday morning as Mother headed off to church, I dared to sneak into her room.

Rummaging through her pretty jewelry, eating the stashed candy tucked neatly away in between her perfumes and make-up, I locked eyes with her deadly weapon.

This small artillery that was not to be discovered, touched, or handled had intrigued my being.

Many times in secret, I've seen Mother in possession of her restricted contraband.

She handled this temptation with care, gripped it in a manner of delicateness, and caution. It was quite a fragile object.

An incorrect maneuver of your finger can cause it to create a mishap. This devil of a device that satisfied my mater when utilizing it, attracted an inner desire that would compel me to risk being caught.

Ultimately succumbed by an intense urge, I seized the weapon, stroked it against my skin, and instantly rue the moment its heat discharged. Never suspecting that one quick blow would change the outcome in my life.

Tranced in a cloud of smokiness, time slipped away and Mother returned. Expeditiously, I flung the weapon at her feet.

A stream of tears ran down our faces, both realizing the grave mistake of possessing this contraption; causing a rift in our flesh, our livelihood, our mere existence.

We allowed our bodies to plummet to our knees and promised that we'll never smoke again.

Summer Vacation

I have left on my summer vacation
With a great and deep depression
An unhappiness in which I cannot hide,
Because it was very hard to say goodbye.
Now I'm far away from you,
And it makes me cry.
Just to say that I miss you.
I yearn for you every day that goes by
And it proves to me,
That my love has not died.
While I'm gone, I will think about you each day
And pray that your love will not fade away.
I know it won't though.
For I trust you.
What I am trying to say is wait for me,
Because I Love You!

Experience Love

In your absence, I feel blue
Because I'm used to seeing just you
I love to see your baby brown eyes.
They are so romantic and keep me hypnotized.
I feel ever so wanted and adored.
Proving that you're not taking my love for granted.
If you were, it wouldn't make a difference to me,
Because I see you and there isn't any other I want to see.
I know that your love is good and real
A love that needs to be concealed.
Our love is something that we like to receive and believe;
And not just give.
Love is an experience that we cannot beat, for it comes in a two-way street.
It's something you give and take, all for real and not fake.
I suggest you take it for real.
So you can express to your partner how you really feel.
Because love is considered to be a chance;
A chance of togetherness to enjoy the experience of romance.

Listen

You talk to me
And I hear your heart
For as long as we love,
We'll never part.
You're so loving, so sweet
So Tender, so Dear,
The Love in your heart
It's all I wish to hear
So don't ever leave me,
Don't go away.
Follow my heart
And listen to what it has to say.

BINGO

Be in no greater obstacle than to love with no regrets, make love on rainy days, foolishly laugh with one another, and remember embrace like it's the last time you'll touch

Be in no greater obstacle that to be there to hold one's hand while in despair, cry silently with a smile remembering the good times, and catch each other's falls when life trips you up.

Be in no greater obstacle than to sleep side by side with bare touches, cuddle and caress to soothe the soul, and the privilege to grow old together.

Be In No Greater Obstacle!

The Day Will Come

Ever since you disappeared away very far,
I came to notice what type of man you really are.
You are a kind of man that cannot be held down, you just follow every pretty girl you see anywhere from uptown to downtown.
All you want are a few nights of pleasure, then you leave them hanging, like an old piece of treasure.
After you get what you want by force, you don't care because we cannot do anything when worse comes to worse.
Again you leave without having a trace to follow you by, and I know you know the reason why.
Soon enough you may meet us in your path again one day, and you're going to wish you are not the one to blame.
When that time comes, your days will be thru, and you won't have any time to know who is who.
All you know is that we gained up on you, and that so-called career of yours is through.
Afterwards we will go our peaceful ways to make a grand celebration while you be in Hell destined to a life of Damnation.

Captured Glance

Captured by a glance, you knew I would be yours
No interest of love, no friendship
What did I foresee in that captivated glance?
Didn't know it at the time, but your smile was as big as your heart.
The way you looked at me, beyond the stare, to my soul.
Never admit that ensnared glance would wake my soul from a dormant state.
Energized my heart to pump a little faster and make my lips sing songs of love and happiness.
You captured my glance, you gazed into my eyes and began a journey through my soul.
I, too, captured a glance.

That Night

Spontaneous circumstances was our introduction
Not knowing your existence
Routinely in our world of undefined blessings
What a lovely sight it turned out to be
That night was cold, crisp, but beautifully still
Allowing our eyes to sparkle in the moonlight
Unfamiliar conversation, exploring unspoken suggestions
To feel secure, without losing all hope of capturing love in the night
Love, the backbone of our being, our destiny.

Love Hurts

You love me, you care for me, but yet you make me cry, you make me doubt.
Examining every angle of my life, ensuring no success, only distress and regrets.
You love me, you care for me, but yet you bruise me, annihilate me, and hate me.
Destroying dreams, wakening demons, unable to wish upon a star.
You love me, you care for me, but yet you dismiss my pleas, you antagonize me.
Living in fear, on pins and needles, hoping no mistakes occur, you dissuade my tears.
You love me, you care for me, but yet you criticize my beauty, you guide my emotions into despair.
Clouding my mind with appalling memories, you blackened every silver lining.
You love me, you care for me, but yet no music jazzes through my soul, no symphony in my heart.
An awaiting life of trickery, you tarnish any hope of a new beginning.
You love me, you care for me, whispering sweet nothings in my ear, rendering a mirage of faded wishes.
Termination of life, detesting the unwelcomed chance, to maybe forever sleep,
Lightly weep, and accept defeat.
You love me, you care for me, but yet with you, the enemy, life and love was temporary.

A Boy

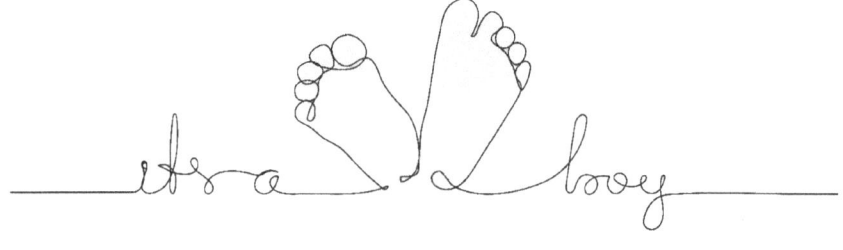

Have you ever wondered, why I love you so?
Have you ever wondered, I guess you don't know.
You've entered my life and filled me with joy.
Then abruptly left, when you found out I was having your boy.
I never knew you were capable of such a thing.
Guess I better not expect the ever wonders that life may bring.
You've shattered my dreams and formed a scar.
But what do you care, you picked up and left in your car.
Oh, I guess I'm on my own again.
Alone with my boy.
However, pardon me for saying:
"Hope in life you never again enjoy."

Lost My Love

Our love meant so much to me, but now it's drifting apart.
So I will let it be since there is no more love in your heart.
I tried to hold on tight, but you got loose again.
I didn't put up a fight because of the tremendous pain.
My tears fell flat on my face, but you didn't seem to care.
You left my room, a place we both have shared.
When you walked out the door without a single goodbye,
I dropped to the floor.
And all night, I CRIED.

Wrong Love

If loving you is wrong, why should I keep holding on?
Everything I do reminds me of you, and I can't believe that what happened is true.
I remember when you put your arms around me and the world would disappear, you would help me forget about my worries and fears.
But now I see that all is gone, and it's all because of wrong love.
It was wrong for me to fall in love with you because all the promises and hopes were not coming through. When I realized the situation at hand, I knew then, that you weren't the right man.
The more I thought about it, the more I cried. Now I understand the reason why. You left without a word of goodbye. I know you realized that our love was wrong, but you had no right to carry on.
If you would've told me about it then, this relationship would not have had an end.
Because I could have been just a friend, until the right moment came for us, one day again.

Winning a Heart

Winning your heart would mean a great deal to me.
I don't care about the obstacles I go through to be with thee.
I know our love will be tender and sweet. Even at a Love Race, it won't be beat.
It will always stay number one because deep in my heart I know that I have won.
I have won your heart at my own pace, racing against time to face you again.
I can stand before you and say that it's true.
The truth is, I am in love with you.
I love you, and I don't care who finds out because it's between you and me.
And baby, that's what it's all about.

Catch Love

It's great to be in love with passion and care.
When nothing above, seems to be there.
You're being swept off your feet and you don't understand.
That all this excitement and joy and heat is determined by your lover
A MAN!

This World

The world is too much with us.
It's like everything seems to be a great big fuss.
Everywhere you go, you might be blamed, and if you don't take caution, you may be framed.
In this world, you have to be in alert, it's like having a boy looking up your skirt.
You cannot be too sensitive or too naïve because sure enough you will be deceived.
If you think everything is supposed to go your way, you better think again as some people may say.

Love Still Blossoms

A church filled with flowers
A bride blooming with roses
The nervous groom awaiting
The union of two hearts
The separateness of two bank accounts
A prenuptial agreement
Waiting in the wings
But LOVE STILL BLOSSOMS
Mothers-in-law waiting to criticize
Grandchildren to be fought over
But LOVE STILL BLOSSOMS
Eyes glued to a football game
Hand stuck to the remote
The shadow of the cook in the kitchen
But LOVE STILL BLOSSOMS
Divorce? Affair? Communication was the missing link
The key to a successful marriage
But LOVE STILL BLOSSOMS!

Endorse with a Kiss

When you fall in love, don't you feel you're upon a cloud?
When you fall in love, does it seem that you want to scream out to the world real loud?
When you fall in love, it's one of the best things that will ever happen to you.
When you fall in love, there is nothing you can't do.
When you fall in love, you're in all these different love tunnels.
When you fall in love, nobody knows…
But, baby, please don't change the channel.
When I must simply say that I have fallen in love him.
I am hoping he has too.
If you have, please kindly endorse with a kiss.

Thinking of You

While I watch the birds sing
All of them so happily
I sit beside my window
Feeling oh so sadly
Thinking throughout the day
That you're miles away
Knowing that you are free
And maybe not thinking of me
It really worries me from time to time
But I know that you are always in my heart
And hopefully will never part.

Having You

The pain I went through to bring you into this world was the most pleasurable sensation I ever felt
The feeling of having something that was mine, the experience of all experiences yet to come
The eternal and maternal warmth and love that only your small, innocent body could bring out of me
Now, as I lay here the only part of me that feels strong is that same eternal and maternal love for you
Those same feelings I had on your first day, will remain with me on my last.

Being Yours

Being yours is having a love I never had before.
Being yours is the eternal love I hold for you forever more.
Being yours helps the love that I give to you never to become sore.
Being yours is not going to be a dream that will not last and become
    a great bore.

Get Out of My Heart

Take that man out of my heart because if you don't, he will tear it apart.
After what he did, I won't accept him back, so he better just leave and face the facts.
I could get hurt for as long as I let it, need to stop it for it holds no merit.
I know well enough that I love the guy, but I also know when to say goodbye.
The pain will take a while to heal, but that won't change the way I feel.
The feelings I felt for him will never return, for all of them have just been burned.
So the day will come when the pain will disappear, and I'll be on a searching tour with a great cheer.
When I find that other guy, I'll make sure he isn't like you because
I know then that the relationship will be new, pretty, and true.

Missing Your Love

Being away from your heart
Really scares me.
Makes me think you want to part
And fill me with misery.
You said our love was true
That nothing could ever come between us.
That it's all about me and you
Also the future but not the past that was
Us being together is very cute
That is how a relationship should look
Caring about each other and giving your love the best
And that's going to be the remedy of your love test.

Serious Love

Always take love very seriously because if you don't it will hurt you deeply.
Love is something you have to be prepared for; otherwise, you will lose and never score.
The way to score a love is to be yourself and not pretend to be anyone else.
If you're not, it would be for the worse.
And definitely blown out of course
Remember, your partner will love you for who you are unconditionally because
He knows your love is true and the rest will be pure and new.
So don't play the game of hard to get, or soon enough you will regret.
And all the love you gain will come out in pain and it will be you to fully blame.
So I will tell you again to take love very seriously, you will come out winning, and won't have an enemy.

I Miss You

I did not think that while away I will miss you, but I guess I was totally wrong.
I've missed you like an uncharged heart missing its beat.
When I heard your voice over the phone, my tears came down as if there was no tomorrow.
Confirming that my days without you are full of sorrow.
Listen, we're miles away from each other; but anywhere I am at, I know our love is true.
Because there's nothing better than you loving me and I loving you.
I cannot wait to be in your arms again, I pray tomorrow will be the day.
I miss you!

Awaiting Your Departure

The many sleepless nights that I have endured
Wishing you depart from my heart and soul.
Countless prayers and wishes adjoin with
Heartfelt tears and sorrow.
Anticipating the moment of freedom,
Awaiting to embrace the new love affairs without permanent connections.
Is this just a dream that will never exist?
Or an illusion that will never cease?
How I wish this awful mirage would materialize itself
I ache when I sleep, dream, imagine, and pray.
The far-fetched conclusion to my nightmare will remain forever a blueprint,
Never to be consummated into a beautiful masterpiece.

Insensitive Love

Life was complete the day you entered my life
Welcomed you with open heart and arms
I just knew you were the one for me

Insensitive when friends smirk as we pass by
Ultimately swore I never leave you
Did not care if you weren't rich or drove a car
I loved you unconditionally

Insensitive when phone did not ring after midnight
Never indicated uncontrollable yearnings
Relationship seemed flawless, no worries
I should have known; it was too good to be true.

Insensitive when held hands depart upon arrival.
Never pictured you to be the villain of my heart.
To destroy all of what we built together as time passed on.
I will never love again.

Insensitive when no kiss given upon going to bed
Unconscious to our needs
Oblivious to our shared plans and secrets
Neglectful to me, your one and only

Insensitive when "I'm sorry" is never spoken.
I loved you with my eyes closed!

Side-View Mirror

Rubbing her eyes, she peered at the blurred caption, "Objects in mirror are closer than they appear."
This statement was clearly interpreting her life as musings were slowly dissipating from view.
The white picket fence with the cracked trellis, a reminder of her broken heart.
The red fire hydrant with the water dripping from its spout, an indication of the countless teardrops.
The crater-shaped pothole that she always forgets to avoid, a warning of the emptiness in her soul.
Continuing to navigate down memory lane, she manages to capture every nuance of her environment.
The ominous dark clouds gathering overhead while a rainbow formed on the edge of the sky.
The complexion of the atmosphere helped find her calm.

Terminating all thoughts, concluding that change was inevitable, she turned once again towards the convex looking glass.

Final view of a rusted weathervane with its snapped arrows, pointing to a fresh start.

No longer to ogle the vexing side-view mirror and its staled memories.

Wanting to Cry

Behind my eyes are buckets full of tears waiting to bawl over
Yet I'd managed to suck them in.
Try not to show the whole world, how much pain I am in.
What can they do?
Give me advice, pray, and treat me with the care of a newborn baby.
I walk slowly through my journeys, bumping into no one, alone is where I want to be.

Yet the tears come down and I cannot help it.
I wipe them away and hope that no one had seen me cry.
For it's an attention for others and an invasion to me.
Don't pay no mind, one day the sun will shine again for me.

Then someone asks, "How are you doing?"
My throat gets tight, my body quivers, and my awaiting tears are dying to bawl over once again.
Can't somebody help me?
No. I have to find a solution on my own.
The world will keep on rotating and the grass will still be green, so what choice do I have but to keep on, moving on.
Till my sunny bright journey return.

However, no matter what, behind my eyes are buckets full of tears waiting to bawl over.

Men and Women

Why is it easy for some men to be insensitive towards women's feelings?
Having the audacity to demand high expectations and selfish demands.

Why can't some women be respected and appreciated for their accolades?
Bearing children, producing mother's milk, or simply asking for directions.

Ever stop to wonder why neither party can be without one another?
Whether it's love, lust, friendship, or even the occasional fling; there's a connection.

Together we need to live, love, experience, and learn. Why continue to outdo one another for neither species is better than.

Regardless of the response, there's no right or wrong answer.

It's a matter of understanding that men and women were created differently, but have the same dominance and attentiveness to cohabitate.

Pledge

Pledge to me the power of your love, house my heart in your soul
Adhere to drafted vows outlining our unquestionable romance
Unwilling to disobey the covenant that bound us together.

Pledge to me that no other will burglarize our committed bond
Acknowledge the untiring efforts set forth for a successful union
To overlook affections, desires, and passion is to rend our promise.

Pledge to me that we'll weather the storm that travel through our paths
Communicate without surly expressions and exercise caution to our feelings
Eliminate reckless behavior and allow pleasantness to prevail.

Pledge to me your trust and I will pledge mine
Yearn for my touch for I will pine for yours
Avow not to veer from our engagement and honor our sworn oath.

This World of Ours

Stop to look at this world of ours, full of pain, love, sickness, and sorrow.
Nobody ever wanted it this way. But it is, needless to say.
Walk down the street, noticing people look depressed, sad, all out of sorts
Unable to determine if they are lonely, unwanted, or stressed. Faces of distort.
Life is nothing but a bowl of cherries, all of them together in a perfect fit
But little do we see that life can be the pits.
Don't get me wrong life is not sour, but it isn't all that sweet neither
But what we can do freely is pray for change
Because this world is still ours.

Caved In

The walls of the cave are crumbling down slowly
Prayer is the only hope.
Breathlessness. No outlet in sight
The entrance that once resided, vanished from existence.
Where did it go? Why am I by myself?
Friends journeying with me are now on the other side of the cave;
Free.
Demoralized in silence, looking for an exit
The darkness, my new companion, never so close were we.

"Why Aren't You with Us?"

On your day of celebration, the sun shined brightly,
But the rays were not shining on you.
The world around was gay.
"Why aren't you with us?"
I tried speaking to you, but you were as deaf as the air.
Your eyes wandering as if they had engaged in a hypnotic state of mind.
The festivity was still going on.
"Why aren't you with us?"
Your body was separated from the rest of humanity.
Your smile imitated the one as the Mona Lisa.
There was no way getting through to you.
"Why aren't you with us?"
I can't really tell if you need my help.
If assistance is needed, don't hesitate to ask.
Just left me with the ongoing question of,
"Why aren't you with us?"

Forgive Me

Forgive me for my faults that seem to follow my life.
Forgive me for my insecurities that have caused you hurt and pain.
Forgive me for my dependence on you.
It can be hard to bare.
I love you, and I'm sorry for any mistakes I have made.
But remember that my heart needs your smiles and laughter.
My soul needs your friendship and love and I need you.

Color

You are not my sister
You don't understand what
It's like walking in a store
Be followed and not be judged
By the colors that you wear,
Credit cards I use and the color
Of my skin

Black and white are beautiful colors.
Can't we see the bride of light?
Not the groom of night.
To understand that we are all the same inside.
All of us.
No matter the color wrapped around
Our bodies

However, one waits as you and I wait,
For a dream in a pocket
Clutching tight, the knuckles of your
Hands, White.
A dream that needs to be awakened

Soon.

Friendship

Friends are forever, whether far or near.
I think of your friendship though you are not here.
As an ode to our fellowship, the stars above shine
The moon gives its glow, the heaven combined.

A friendship should not be taken for granted.
I give great thanks for ours being so true.
I value your friendship and treat it as treasure.
My acquaintance with you.

Our companionship valued more than silver or gold.
This is a friendship that was not bought,
Nor can it be sold.

So I say, my dear friend, though miles keep us apart
You're with me every day,
In my thoughts and my heart.

This is not goodbye
Long years may pass us by
Our friendship will last
To lighten and brighten
Whatever life's clouds may try and hide.

Unable to Say Goodbye

A tear I cry when I have to say goodbye;
The heartbreak and pain, are to one's gain.
The love we shared, all the things we feared.
One final goodbye, made me break down and cry.
The love we had was special to me, forever together in my mind we'll be.
To live alone is not what I do, I'll always have thoughts of you.
The moments we spent sharing our dreams, the laughter, I remember, as yesterday it seems.
My lovely cries are dark and loud without your love, I'm never proud
To think back happily to an old memory, I love you, only you, and no other I see.
Yes, I love you so, I can't let go.
I'm holding on tight, the lonely nights, the restless days I remember back to all our old days.
My tears fall, a message they say,
Until you return, I'll wait till that day.

In This Park

In this park that I dwell, I met the guy I loved so well.
He came and stole my heart from me, now he's gone, he set me free.
He sat this girl on his knee, he told her things he never told me.
Now I know the reason why. She was prettier than I.
I ran straight home to my bed, not a word to Mother was said.
My father came home later that night, search for me from left to right.
Up the stairs and to my room, he found me hanging from a rope.
On the dresser there was a note:
"Dig me a grave and dig it deep, where all the marbles cover me from head to feet.
On the stone please place a dove to show the world I died for LOVE."

It Only Hurts Now

Don't look back
When you head for the door
Because if you do
It'll only hurt more
Don't stop to explain
Don't tell me why
If you're going to leave
Just say goodbye
I love you, I miss you
But I can make it alone
I want you, I need you
But I can hold my own
Because I can't tie you down
You've got to be free
And I can't make you love only me.
So don't look back, I'll tell you again
Just say goodbye, if this is the end.

Please Tell Me

Unconditional love is an experience of a lifetime
The love that can be admired and cherished, along with being hated and negated
The adaption of habits, moods, and the art of loving someone other than yourself.
Is that hard to achieve?

Please tell me.

Looking out of windows, walking down streets, and people illustrating love in an easy, romantic fashion with no hesitations.
Is that a fairy tale?

Please tell me.

Even if told, love is not forever
I will welcome it with open arms
For our hearts will conquer all uncertainties and create an everlasting bond
Is it all a lie?

Please tell me.

Yesterday

Yesterday we cried, in each other's arms.
For our lost love, for our inexplicable harm.
Yesterday we loved, pure and true.
You loved for me, I loved for you.

Passing Love

I didn't expect to see you there, with your warm eyes and dark hair.
You hung around with your friends, my imagination ran with no end.
I watched you carefully so you wouldn't see, my heart in my throat, my eyes traitor to me.
Then came the time I looked at the clock above, I had to leave.
Leave my passing love.

Little Bird

Oh, little bird so small and blue.
When will you sing only for you?
Such a sweet, rich sound you use each day.
Sweeping my cares and blues away.
Sing to me little bird so I will never forget.
That I gave all my love, but none did I get.

Love

Love is sharing,
Love is caring,
Love is always kind.
Somehow when I think of you,
It's you that's on my mind.

Lonesome

Is being alone all that bad?
Is having friends a passing fad?
I'm alone but I don't feel alone;
No one's at the door or on the phone.
Some people might say, being alone day by day
Is boring as a rainy day in May.
I am not ashamed to be by myself, for I will not depend on anyone
    else.
So I tell you, friend, it's not that bad being alone.
Besides, I know it won't be for very long.

Earth

When I am in my room staring at the walls,
I think about the world and her downfalls.
The world we live in is not all it's cracked up to be
That's why it needs understanding from people like you and me.
You and I, together, can take it as it is
And live in it, with anger or bliss.

Despite its controversies, this world may remain the same,
But if we do nothing, we're really to blame.
We can try and give just a little to make it better
Or leave it to the rest of the nincompoops to shred her.
We know we can make this a greater place
And when we do, this world can be embraced with no disgrace.

Special Someone

Loving someone special is like being on a cloud,
No one to be near, no one around.
It's being kind, tender, so sweet,
That is why love will sweep me off my feet.
People may compare it to puppy love,
I may consider it, but it's as beautiful as a dove.
Being in love is a once-in-a-lifetime experience,
It's not being full of blindness, but being in remembrance.
It will open a new life in me, something I never let to be free.
It made the bad things in life, into good things,
No matter the problems that life brings.
To me it's the sweetest thing in the land,
Imagine just holding hand in hand.
I know in the future I won't be a rue, but in the meanwhile,
I hope all my dreams come true.
Let's talk about me and you.

The Call

Dawdling down the beach
I stared deep into the profound blue sky
The ocean waves splashing against
The jetty and all of a sudden
I started to cry.
I cried in silence for not a
Tear would fall,
And looked at the Heavens as if that
Someone would call.
I needed to hear a call.
A call from beyond; a call
That no one else would give ear to.
But as I sat there—waiting
I felt a sudden fear.
Quickly, I came back from my
Hypnotic trance
And thought to myself,
You're searching for a call that is hard to hear.
So I strolled and I strolled
With my shadow following me so tall,
And mumbled to myself,
Will I ever hear the call?

Secret Admirer

He always writes me letters
Leaving them unsigned
He never calls during the day
Always in the night
His name is unknown to me
His face is a mask
I always dream of him
And hope my dreams would last
One day I'll meet him and
He will take my hand
My secret admirer and
I will build our own dreamland.

At First

At first I hated you, then I met you
I didn't know you, but then I liked you
I admired you for a while, and I started to care
I doted on you a great deal, but one day
I loved you.

I adored you for a long time and you were mine,
For a long time I just cherished you, and
Now I love you forever
I'll always love you, only you
Unconditionally
Because nothing will ever separate
You and me.

Hand in Hand

Hand in hand they walked in love
Of lovely things they talked
Mostly of sharing time alone with each other.

Hand in hand they smiled in love
Enjoying each other's presence
She loved his eyes, he loved her essence.

Hand in hand they reminisce in love
Thinking of what tomorrow will bring
Neither seems distraught that the season was not Spring.

Hand in hand they matured in love
Growing up together, trying not to smother
Learning on how to dote on one another.

Hand in hand they aged in love
Living, loving, and laughing.
Embracing each other in their arms forever, hand in hand.

Love on My Nerves

I'm desperate in love
I feel my world caving in.
I'm always thinking of him,
He's so cool but conceited.
Sometimes I find him looking at me
Strangely with an inexplicable expression.
If he loves me, he'll never say it
I'll probably never know
Love can get on my nerves.

Him

Who always looks deep in my eyes?
Keeping me ever so memorized.
Him

Who smiles and fills my heart?
Hoping we will never part.
Him

Who holds my heart in his palm?
Hypnotizing me with his charm.
Him

Who is the subject of my dreams?
Envisioning our wedding.
Him

Who would I choose as my Prince Charming?
Praying that it would last forever.
Him

Forever Love

Remembering all the good times we had makes me happy and also sad.
To think of all the good times we shared and now we have nothing to spare.
The things we promised and loved would still be a secret up above.
Even though we drifted apart we'll still be in each other's heart.
Our love with tender loving care, will never go away, it will always stay there.

Alone

Why do I get this feeling, it's like I'm alone
Nobody by my side, no one to call my own.
If I could have a lover, so we could hold each other
Or a friend I can call on the telephone.
My girlfriend tells me there's someone in the world for me
I'm looking high and low, this man I can't seem to see.
Soft zephyr whirling unknowingly
Never to blow a love for me.
Why do I have this feeling? I hate to be sad
My enemies like to tease me, it makes me mad.
They say I'll die alone
With never a one to miss me when I'm gone.
And I'll keep on wishing for this love I never had
Desperately hoping to remove myself from the want ads.
Maybe being alone is always for the best
I'll get lucky and find a guy unlike the rest.
It's not so lonely but I want somebody next to me.
I'll keep you in my heart and treasure your love truly.

Zippered

Eyes sealed, unable to catch sight of falling tears
Lips stitched, unspoken lyrics never to be uttered
Ears tucked, unavoidable whispers never to be forgotten
Mouth closed, unescapable words never to be declared
To reveal this love within my soul may result in treason
Betrayal to my feelings and surrender to a loveless existence.

If charged, condolences to my heart.

Rebel without a cause, a loner forced to embrace an unforgivable secret
A form of blasphemy, submerged in guilt.

An acquitted beloved, hypocrite to our love, set free to pursue its desired passion
Unrequited love, forsaken to a broken heart, flat-lined.

Zippered eyes
Zippered lips
Zippered ears
Zippered mouth

Blind, voiceless, deaf, and mute.

By Chance

We met by mutual circumstances
A nonchalant handshake and a coy smile
Although not impressed to meet each other
Our eyes were unable to deny the immediate attraction.

He has all the hallmarks of a great lover, and
I all the complications of a well-seasoned woman
My heart beating raucously through my body,
Giving away my fiery desire to make him mines
His sexual tension so palpable, hardly unnoticeable
To the naked eye, making him more irresistible.

Life has a whimsical sense of humor
A serendipitous encounter for our unbeknownst rendezvous
Free from strife, able to want you without it being a necessity
A welcoming option, rather than a priority.

No longer starved by physical touch
Satisfied on all cylinders, unleashed to a gentle lover
Reconciling my conscious, without constraints.
Time-stamped in the moment
No scheduled engagements
An afterthought, uninterrupted in time, and
Indefinitely in our minds.

Shattered

Love is not perfect
You were my beginning and my end
Forgave unforgettable things under duress
Countless times of compromise with no appreciation or rest.

In my eyes you were the one, my heart needed no failsafe
Requiring no backup for a malfunction
Detected no threat to my heart
No mention of assumptions.

My broken transponder
Struck by a loveless arrow, Cupid unable to resuscitate
I loved you wrong because I knew no better
Now a lifeless cadaver, renouncing love altogether.

Patently obvious love is not to blame
Active participant you were in my heartbreak
Equally accountable for our spoiled connection
The bane to my existence, a parasite, an infection.

Exanimated to embracing love once more
Open arms to another shot at love
Not to be welcomed without scrutiny whatsoever
Next time around, it will be my last and forever.

Hell's Kitchen

Standing in the middle of the scullery
Where drenched in sweat you baked with love all my desires
Though our relationship was a recipe for disaster
The whirlwind affair blew up in smoke, nothing left of the fire.

Our menu served hot and heavy kisses, blended with vigorous coitus
Scent of our bodies permeated through the air
Melding with the aroma of sweet and spicy fragrances
Arising temperatures only to deflate in despair.

Pickled off of your love, my lips parched, and soul famished
Hankering to knead your heart and jam it with the love you once
    knew
The intimacy that marinated us together, and also skewed us apart
Left with a chilled space, charred memories, no longer anything to
    infuse.

No need to flee from love, scorched ashes can rekindle a spark
Either way left alone, unstirred, bland, an inedible gourmet
Not off the market quite yet, an appetite to acquire
Seize new spice, dollop a fresh taste, toast a drink, and indulge in a
    buffet.

Ingredients for a steamy romance
Where no time can be measured
Apply generous amount of heat
Thickly throughout our layers of love
Love-proofed.

By Invitation Only

This part of my life is by invitation only
Definitely worth the price of admission
Screaming at the past
Tripping over my future
Knowing the reality of my truth.

Removed from the lost and found
Exhausted by unearthing the unnecessary
Conundrums no longer on repeat
Understanding the value of thy self.

Place a bid and hope to obtain access
For the truest one who loves my soul may enter
Vacancy for emotional bail out available
Only subscribing to those with reservation.

Custom-made to be a part of a forever couple
Discontinuing the search of yesterday
Accepting the today
Unknowingly anticipating tomorrow
Awaiting my destiny by invitation only.

Seasonal Hazard

How do I tell my heart you might not be coming back?
You won't be kissing my lips or touching my hands
Emotions crippled by your absence, falsifying a heart attack.

I have a love that only feeds on your voice
At an impasse, unsure of petitioning for your love
Wishing you return to me by choice.

The Seasons will come and go in intervals
Days will turn to night and time will no longer revert
The year will continuously pass me in circles.

Everyone does not remain unchanged
A man needs no permission from his heart to love
Submissive to his emotions, feelings unexplained.

Apprehended by thoughts, risking it all to passion
The hazards of missing you in all Seasons

Remembering how our love blossomed in the SPRING
Followed by steamy love-making nights in the SUMMER
Holding hands in FALL ensued by tight bear hugs
Bundling by a cozy fireplace in the WINTER
Dreaming of the day we become Mr. and Mrs.

Perfect Imperfections

Imperfect couples enjoy their differences
Love is uniquely wrapped for everyone
Appreciating the slight curves that bulge on our hips
Fascinated by the odd slope of our noses.

Invisible to many in a crowded place
Baffled by the fact that there's so much we have in common
Missed opportunity on your part
I may well be the Ying to your Yang, the shortstop to your second
    base.

Beauty has always been in the eye of the beholder
Refresh your mind and give it a whirl
Partake in the imperfections that surround you
Consider love as your best friend, an accomplice, your lover.

Delete the current version of yourself
Adopt a new way of loving others
Overdose in the moment, take a risk
Submerge in love as if a witch has cast a magic spell.

Real love is the one where you feel alive inside
Regardless of how many times it took you to get there
If my imperfections are perfect for you
Reject the ordinary
Live and let go
When love feels right, leave all the nonsense behind.

"Lovectomy"

Fear of unrequited love was my Achilles heel
The rejection caused my heart to ache
Desperately seeking for a diagnosis to my pain
Only for a doctor to disclose the removal of her love from my heart.

Our love was toxic, contaminated,
But benign
Contagious to no one, emotionally scarring me for life
No amount of sutures can repair the loss of her touch
Failing with no remedy to this sickness
Romantically flat-lined.

Never will I operate the same without her
Self-restrained, no backbone
To continue fighting this one-sided romance
No consultation needed
To know that her heart was dormant to my needs
Lack of loving me granted the award-winning prize of the lone survivor.

Alone, no prescription to heal this unhopeful prognosis
Don't need discharge papers to tell me that I'm in remission
To breathe a sigh of relief, to follow up with another love
STAT…
Remain optimistic that love never dies.

Ms. Sery

Teardrops saturating my pillow as I lay awake
Drowning in my own sorrow
Knowing that I am everything you think
You never needed
Nonetheless, what wouldn't I do, for you to be my
Prince and wipe away my tears.

Not peddling fairy tales or wearing a mask
What you see is what you get
Wished I'd listened to my heart and
Swiped left
Yet keeping my fingers crossed
Pleading you'd give us a chance.

My assurances don't satisfy the skeptic
Gleam in your eyes.
Take a good look at me
The glass slipper may not be my size
But we fit perfectly together.

Break the spell
Let's show off the beauty of our love
And release the beast within us
And live happily ever after.

When Love Leaves You

If I could turn back the hands of time
Return to the past
To the day before I met you
Then I wouldn't have to say goodbye.

No one stops to let death thru
But it happened, he came for you
Not nearly ready to bid you farewell
Now you're faded from view
No choice but to raise a glass of Zinfandel.

Dreaming of you in a restless sky
Where stars roam free and bright
Knowing you no longer dream in color
Half of my heart gone
Living aimlessly in black and white.

I'll light a candle and promise not to cry
Such heartache, wish I had more time
At the foot of your grave
Facing the sunrise with you
I'll stay until the sun sets
Whispering a regrettable adieu.

Damn You

Damn, I want all my years back
The times when I was your chef, nurse, maid,
Cheerleader, and freak in the bed
I want it all back with interest.

How dare you make me feel so deranged?
Unable to focus, inconsistent to my own needs
Verbal bruises covered up by a pseudo smile
Inundated in misery, realizing that it was never love, but lust.

Love is not supposed to hurt, yet here I am
Abandoned with souvenirs of mistrust and insecurities
Hearted you with all my might, but it was never my duty to do so
Concierge to my emotions, need to leave and mend my broken soul.

Facing the truth, a scarred reflection looking back at me
And where are you? Did you even care?
Time wasted, overdue for a break, no longer sitting around for better days
The source of my irritation, but admitting you were my favorite mistake.

The hardest thing is letting go
Running far away with newfound sage, never to find another like you
Someday you'll miss me, and I won't be there to witness
Should have loved me when you had the chance,
I don't give a damn now,
Just scram!

News Feed

Breaking news
No longer making personal appearances in your life
Sources inform me that you're in love with someone else.

Downloaded my heart and soul into our relationship
While you interfaced with another in public
An updated version perhaps, but definitely not me.

Enjoy the limelight with your new fling
You'll soon realize that her feedback is incomparable to mines
Fool me only once, this site is no longer available.

Scammer to my heart, virus to my essence
My brain reeling under the impact of this news
I've changed the channel, love not to be taken for granted.

Return to sender
You're type has been deleted
Keep scrolling, notyourbuffoon.com deactivated.

History won't repeat itself
Linked-in to someone who enjoys my platform
Minute-by-minute love, audience of one
A blockbuster pay-per-view special event.

XOXO approved

Faux Love

Our love was based on a promise
A pinky swear to only love one another wholly
No guarantees of success
A preliminary draft to a story narrated by us.

Love in our eyes, hope in our hearts
Never thinking of an unhappily ever after
But the ink dried fast and the page is now blank
No written words to attest our fairy tale.

Hard to conceptualize that a white lie ruined our novella
Concocted words followed by fake hugs and kisses
Unbind by the coil that bound us as one
Tears smear the words of love that once stained the page.

You were just supposed to be a chapter in my story
False protagonist temporarily plagiarizing the narrative
Telling the truth even when lying mitigates the pain to my soul
Tethered by hollow pretense.

Shutting the book on this shamble of a romance
No placement holder to indicate a return
A defunct plot that would be remembered only
If history repeats itself.

Ignorance is at most bliss when the truth
Is covered by an illustrated façade
Anonymous to thy heart.

False Ring

Can't wait for life to stop being hard to be happy
Treating me as your past but supposed to be your future
We fell in love and created soul ties
Hopeful of a happy life, possible wife, and all its sacrifice.

Absence makes the heart grow fonder
Always chasing the one that got away
While I stand here offering you my flesh, my heart, my soul
Fool not to notice that I'm a victim of happenstance.

Truth is…absence makes the heart grow absent
Never thought to be someone's exit
Hard to work it out when the other has options
At no time did I ever place you second.

All of a sudden mincing words is your foreplay
Nothing can be said to remove this bad aftertaste
Selflessly loving you with no regard of rejection
My handicap of being head over heels for you was your prize.

For all that causes hurt makes us broken
No longer your clutch, to catch you when you fall out of love
I meant nothing to you, but you meant everything to me
Left alone with no sparkle of a wedding ring, just gifted with suffeRING.

Mourning Spirit

Patiently waiting for morning to come
Greet the sun with a solemn smile
Wake of emotions restless, seeking an escape
Disregarding the loudness within these silent walls.

Heart overwhelmed with an inexplicable sense of sadness
Gentle breeze embracing my body
The oddities that exist
Blanketed my soul with a familiar presence.

Faint smoky scent, a reminder of an old flame of yesteryear
Dedicated ourselves to love from afar
Love inconsiderate to our needs
Victims of inconvenient timing
No compromise.

Suffused with rhetoric in the air
Moon kissed by the sky
Your shadow lulled to sleep by symphony of stars.

Dreams will reunite our souls
Until it's my moment to squeeze the sky with you.

Monday Loving

When the world is sleeping, I lay in bed staring at your body
Never to imagine a version of life without you
Nothing else matters in this moment
Only to share my love with you because no one else will do.

My body, your body, our bodies
Covered completely in love
Two raw hearts beating as one
Dedicating ourselves into we turn to dust.

My heart is at ease, no reason not to give in to you
Uncover my modesty and let your nature grow
Close your eyes, caress my body, and clench the sheets
Indulge in one another with a climatic cry of release.

Don't let go and pour yourself deeply into me
Let the minutes blur into hours and days to nights
Flirty tongue kissing my undisclosed tattoo
Loving each other from sunset to morning dew.

Our touch awakening our souls
Quenching the thirst that's parched inside us
Your eyes sending a burning sensation and
My body erupting like a volcano drenched in our lava.

Breathe a sigh of relief and know
We'll keep falling in love over and over again
So long as you touch me, hold me, kiss me, and love me.

Drunken Mule

The intoxicated words that slurred from your mouth
Pierced my ears and hurt my core
A drunkard's word more truthful than that of a sober tongue.

Your love is not good for my health
Playing house with a man who doesn't want to create a home
All that we've built, crumbled to the ground.

Home is where the heart is but I have no residency
No longer do I hold the key to your heart
Checking out with a suitcase full of memories.

Left alone to brood in a dark place
Buried with emotions packed on by your ego
Need to escape and leave it all behind.

Love is a journey, steps foreign to our crossroads
No o'clock time restraining me from living
Owe myself an apology for dealing with this bullshit.

Take you as you are or let you be
To live unburdened and get some reciprocity.

The Window

These days I look out the window in hopes to see you again
Dubious to opening it and letting fresh air in
For the staled memories of your presence still curtains the room
Complicating the unmarred view that once stood.

Every day is a different outlook paneled by painful emotions
Turn a blind eye, take a loss, and give up on love
Reframe the mindset and take control
Strip away the tainted karma of your traumatized heart.

This opening in the middle of a wall, an overview of my life
Awaiting a simple gesture of sliding the pane up or down
Allowing a gentle breeze to forecast the emotional struggle of my soul
Weathering the storm to calm my spirit.

My eyes were the windows to your soul
My love awning all insecurities and self-sabotage to the heart
The picture-perfect aspect of our love shattered
Now blurred and unfocused, like the view in a kaleidoscope.

Wipe the stained glass and open the square
Embrace the box that reflects back at me
Sit on the sill and look into my eyes
My window is you.

Interference

You're a distraction!

Thinking of you more times than I care to count
Monopolize my thoughts, being a bother to my heart
No introduction needed, keep on moving
Broken heart not accepting any new solicitation.

Follow the path of past intruders who have tried and failed
Not worth interrupting my heart again to be let down
Determined to safeguard this whirlpool of emotions
Defy the bad influences that will scar me for life.

Camouflage my heart to be hard and cold
Struggling not to succumb to the warm touch of your hand
Withstand the flirt of your tongue whispering sweet nothings in my ear
Resist your public display of affection that is wearing me down.

Unfocused, pondering whether or not to love you back
Vulnerable heart swaying wildly like an uncontrollable pendulum
Realizing that I, too, deserve love and happiness
Learned that a broken heart can heal and be intimate once more.

Disturbance no longer trespassing my being
Caught up in the rapture of our romance
Pursue passion even when times are strained
Treasure each other and promise never to kiss and tell.

Hollow Man

The door was left open but never did you return
Saddened by your abrupt departure
My soul unable to recuperate from a closed heart
No longer looking through the peephole for your homecoming.

You left without a kiss goodbye
Not a word, not a sound, not a whisper
No lip-stained message to raise suspicion
Of the hurt coming my way.

Loved all the pieces that made you whole
But you couldn't love half of me
Treated like a pair of hired hands tirelessly waiting
To be loved back from the one causing my heartbreak.

Trying to laugh to keep from crying
Knowing love should have brought you home
Not homesick enough to address my unhappiness
Willing to replace the key to my heart for another.

No matter which key houses your heart now
Be certain that no one would love you like I do
Selfishly will wait for the day you're unleased
And come back to my open arms where you're meant to be.

Readiness for Love

Your rugged exterior allows one's imagination to fantasize
That heart beats as wild as stormy waves
Your arms welcoming the love for a beautiful woman is
Irresistible and charming
Men who are denied such an experience and pleasure
Can only allow their imagination to fulfill their innocence
Your curiosity embraces:
Readiness for love
Observance to needs
Beautiful in aura
Experiencing life
Realistically inclined
Tempted to invite more love than ever imaginable
Into an empty heart
If ever I may be wrong of this love
So surprisingly embellished
Then never would I regret it
For Miracles don't happen quite often and adventures do stray away
Remember this always:
I will love you for the warmth and tenderness you cherish upon me
And the memories created for uncertain times of loneliness.

Love Welcumed

My heart has unapologetically decided on you
Can't control myself much longer
Passion suffering a prolonged drought
Granting permission to be flooded by your love.

Your body has an aphrodisiac power unable to be resisted
Let endorphins be released and consummate our desires
No longer satisfied by pillow talk
Tension between our bodies is too great.

Take off your clothes and strip down
Dirty thoughts coming to life
Fingers roaming, circling our anatomy
Stirring the primal need within us to be aroused.

Soft strokes of the tongue erecting goosebumps
Moaning and groaning with lust in our eyes
Catch me below drinking your wine
While drowning you in the sweetness of my nectar.

Drank freely the releases of our natural sap
Absorbing the spilled seed inside me
Listening to our rapid heartbeats
Addicted to the drug of our mind, body, and psyche.

Closed Heart

I don't love you the same way that you love me
Honestly believe we were better off as friends
Emotionally jaded by the efforts you impose
Unwilling to betray my heart to please yours.

Love being with you so long as we aren't coupled
No desire to be involved in a romantic entanglement
You claim to understand, but continuously plea for my love
The one thing I'm reluctant to share.

Without doubt, I run the risk of losing you
But what can I do, my stubborn heart won't approve
One day you'll find someone that'll make you happy
Embraced by sadness, I'll let you go, my soul won't disapprove.

No rhyme or reason why I couldn't participate my life with you
Don't want to share my heart, my home, or my bed
Company I most cherish is being alone
Unescorted from a relationship that would not hold its own.

No matter how many times I say goodbye
There are numerous ways you find to say hello
Surrendered to the antics for no more strength endured
You don't listen, but my actions will speak louder than words.

Cuda Bear

Wish you were here to thank you in person
To bow my head and curtsey in your honor
Express the gratitude in my heart
For you birthed the love of my life.

Traveled half a century before getting the chance to meet him
Entertained many rotten apples, disagreeable to the core
Trusted my heart onto unreliable hands
Experiencing mediocre love, no forth effort given.

Prayed every night for that special someone
In my heart of hearts, I knew God engineered one just for me
Laughed and cried throughout the years
Still refusing to give up on love.

What journeys in his life did he embark
Being seasoned just right for me
Experiencing different milestones that paved his path
Letting fate decide, allowing his roads to cross mines.

He was definitely worth the wait
My heart belongs to no one but him
You have a front-row seat to our undying love
Blessed to have it all with the man you raised, just perfect for me.

Retired Yesterday

Not worth the effort reverting to a love you once knew
Intimately abandoned, no forever heart to call your own
Temporary amnesia, only remembering the good times
Soft kisses, holding hands, laying on his chest while taking a nap.

Solitude sacrificed, settling for unwanted company
A naïve heart, cautious mind being disregarded
Sometimes nothing is everything, just let it be
Left for a reason the first time around, take heed.

Your love treated me wrong, a careless passion
Unfaithful heart, disloyal to the relationship
Brokenhearted, cast aside, former lover, present stranger
Thought you could resave my heart, what was I thinking!

Waiting for a sorry or an explanation, Hades will freeze over
Melded hearts now collide, to argue with no compromise
Stop the past from repeating itself, take control
Stabilize your life, recollect what led to this demise.

No longer a bumper sticker, removing the heartless decal
Scraping off unwanted residue of bad experiences
Not sticking around for yesterday's romance
New label stamped, adhesive to today's love only.

Kaleidoscope

Love is the common denominator for all things that exist
Challenges the heart to dream in color
To be unconscious to the black and white
For all of us are tainted within.

Photograph the moments that feel like sunshine
Allow vulnerabilities to touch your heart
Love is not experienced the same way twice
Blanketed by a cascade of kaleidoscopic emotions.

Colorful eye to the soul, an iridescent dimple
Sometimes blindsided by the aura of our moods
Dance on my parade, splash color into the light
Shaded pigments undermined, spurn the monochrome of night.

Every tint, every stain, connects us to a starburst of passion
Copious amount of feelings constantly changing
Mayhem of drunken colors, a color-kissed kryptonite
Colorblind by a medley of fickle affections sieving through our souls.

Coloration of love embraces the artless intimacy of our heart
Restore the torn rainbow, accept your color-stained canvas
Showcase the crayons that survived the darkness
A beautiful sight to behold, a warm caress to the body.

Reserved Love

If I knew then what I know now, I wouldn't have loved you
Red flags flapped loudly, ignored all the warning signs
On top of the world, then the world on top of me
Mutiny of the heart, hard luck, human folly.

Plethora of emotions, hosted by theatrics and masquerade
Never did you truly love me, just a game of Charades
Romantically breadcrumbing my heart, staled, crumbled
Recollected the pieces, tasted teardrops, your name never again mumbled.

As the days don't repeat themselves, neither will my love for you
Passion unsilenced, farewell to the woman that love forgot
Heartless betrayal, still not afraid, plenty of romance preserved
Next silhouette a turnstile away, not hiding, ready to be found.

No rush, soft peddling, not carrying the weight of the past
Fateful oversight, embracing uncertainty, ceased being the jester
Relieved, living again, it doesn't hurt anymore
No more lies, sugar kissed the pain, new pleasure to explore.

Without reluctance, expect the unexpected, reserve an open heart
Don't doubt, push forward, be optimistic, and hug another soul
Stay ready, love births every second, grasp the moment
Not bound by time, love is out there, introduction unknown.

Convicted

Opportunistically lived life by taking advantage of your heart
Exploited all the goodness that it offered
Always on the cusp of staying grounded or disappearing forever
Emotionally distant, self-refraining from any tender touch.

Unloved at birth sight, miscomprehension of intimacy
Afraid of relationships, steadfast confusion, tug-of-war of emotions
Your love questioned my heart, trial and error prevailed
Unwarranted fears, hypothetical to think my soul would yearn endearment.

Uphill battle, each struggle graduated to another struggle
Your presence calmed my inner turmoil, it embraced the endless passion
Recanted promises, welcomed accomplice, thought love was finally on my side
Short-lived, depressed with regret, life convicted me in another direction.

Heart barren, impregnated with sorrow, delivered to darkness
Non-retroactive moment, force to rescind all hopeful expectations
Soul incarcerated to misery, released to lifeless shadows
Forever indebted to you, temporarily animated my soul with tender, loving, care.

The fight is over, no choice but to love you behind steeled bars
On borrowed time, romance overstayed its welcome
Void of emptiness, flighty annoyance, sentence to life without your romance
In solitude with jailed feelings, memories arraigned for visitation in dreams only.

Elevator Surfing

Followed the foot traffic on route to an unfamiliar ride
Trapped in this journey with foreign skins
Ricochet of fragrances nosing throughout the enclosed space
Desperate to find you and return your broken heart.

Bobble-heading left and right, anxious to see you in the crowd
That moment when our eyes interlocked briefly, time stood still
Bodies reluctantly trying not to touch, heart beats accelerated
Split second when a part of us connected, souls tied as one.

Lost track of you, surrounded by an army of frenzied figures
Emotional roller coaster of feelings, connection broken
Nowhere to go, but to the metal box where we first met
Claustrophobic with a vertigo heart, riding time capsules until we
    meet again.

Back against the wall, searching high and low in the faces of strangers
Your absence causing great angst, let me find you, reveal yourself
My soul won't hold more than it can bare, reemerge and revamp my life
I know I don't exist, the pursuit will continue, I'll risk it all for you.

Elevator surfing, unwavering stance, a game of hide-and-seek until I win
Determined to return the half-hearted locket, fallen hastily from
    your neck
A gemmed message to replace the other half of your heart with mine.

    Glanced up and there you were, a sight for sore eyes, willing to surf
        sky scrapers endlessly.

A Diary Page

Don't judge our love by the amount of times we say I love you
Your words carry no weight, overloaded with long-buried pain
Maimed my heart over and over again, you're the logical poison
The familiarity prohibiting me to escape the grip of your toxicity.

Harbored secrets, scars diarized on a failed organ
Collapsed with regret, no electricity in the soul, need to recharge
Go rogue and release the emotions caged like a feral animal
Your heart is not a guest, wear the sweat of your blood as war paint
Double down, dull cynical noises that echo, and fight for custody of
    your being.

The silence in a soul can keep the heart awake, a constant alarm clock
Reminder to fill the empty void, bandage the wounds, emancipate
    the torment
Recollect the broken pieces one at a time, and repair the damage
Inaugurate love once again, be unafraid to lead your heart to unfa-
    miliar chambers.

Happiness matters, love shouldn't be complicated, reject sadness
Some days you have to choose to be your own sunshine
Let not the darkness interfere, embrace your destined crossroad
Be uncomfortable with the comfortable, make it make sense
Celebrate Christmas in July, be the host of your Season.

Self-evict the flummoxed voices, debut of a renewed gentle heart
Outcry the chaos that no longer riots, love more than hate, smile instead of weep
Pine to be carefree, authorize the soul to dance in the rain
Allow the heart to sing, and permit life to continually carry a beat.

Fallen

Please catch me, can't take the pain if I fell again
My mind is tired, exhausted from summersaults of loveless thoughts
Criticized by the way I love you, enduring juvenile rants, being undermined
Microchipped my heart, purposely to discourage other suitors
Unruly bastard with intent on pillaging my heart, desecrate my soul
Determined to break my spirit and assassinate my hopes and dreams.

Fifty shades of tirades, afraid to express trapped anxieties and shame
Destined as a passionless charity, subject to rumor and anecdote
Feeble strength, defenseless to attacks, lost in a wounded heart, helpless
Nothing happens by chance, pathetic performance, wallowed in fear
Bitter juror to my heart, orphan to my being, irrefutable consequences
A nightmare in disguise, doppelganger to my paradise, no relief of euphoria.

Never asked for more than I deserve, maybe I should have, overwhelmed by guilt
Consumed with a man's broken heart, unable to love anyone but himself
Listless love, disheartened, beckoned to misery, overshadowed by dreary twilight
Turned off my mind, eavesdropping on the sound of darkness, a welcomed notion
Alternative joyride to happiness, misbegotten journey, accompanied by loneliness
Hidden tracker disabled, no longer a hostage, liberated from your emotional chaos.

Renege on my plea, don't catch me, and let me fall into the arms of death
Cemented to the ground, in a coffin with no pockets, dying broken but free
Swallowed by a dark hole, blanketed by dirt.

Let me fall into a deep slumber, unable to catch a glimpse of the afterlife.

Gambler

The inconsistent way you touch me, places a seed of doubt in my heart
When glancing at me, no longer do your eyes twinkle in admiration
Inconspicuous roll of the eyes, the shrugged shoulders of disinterest
Sacrificing our years of love, willing to gamble, and risk it all away.

The grass isn't always greener on the other side, sometimes it's dull
Avoid the temptation, bet your bottom dollar on my heart
Grave consequences in the interplay between losing me and winning her
Crap shoot of a decision, stakes are high, is Lady Luck on your side?

In the game of love, don't bet against your heart, quite a rookie move
Quit while you're ahead, anticipate the possibility of a loss
A coin toss, tales you lose, emotions coin flipped by impulse and desperation
Pink slipped your heart with no sign of regret, con artist with a poker face.

Raffled your love away, laying the odds against me, door prize a bust
Rolled snake eyes, forfeited what was right in front of you
Thought you could play the field, bad bet on your part, no straight draw
Dicey turn of events, no longer calling the shots, limited options, sandbagged.

No need for a replay, not calling your bluff, you've broken my slot machine
Tossup of a poor choice, our souls no longer have an algorithm
Played with our love like a game of Roulette that backfired, should of betted on red
True love always wins in the end, no longer my bookie, game over.

A Virgin's Plight

Never planned on losing you
The man who had a hand in the raising of my womanhood
Mapped out by your own personal perspective
Ignorant to the many facets of love, limited to the different colors it offered.
In your presence, love was black and white
Purposely shaded to be plagued by your version of love alone
Heart devoid of romanticism, scarce emotions, dubious delectation
No true betterment in the horizon.
Love is deeper than the embedded scars in my soul
The internal rage of feelings incarcerated in my heart
Panic-stricken, fighting to awaken from an endless ordeal
To bestir oneself and choose to stop falling prey to obscurity.
The unknown is a better decision than you
Time to unshackle and shake the rigor mortis pending abode
At the precipice of discovering passion with another beau
Forbidding the love of a predecessor taint thy harlequin being.
Rise like the Phoenix and lean into love, not obligation
Embrace the one who will do life with you
Love is an uncomplicated word, interpreted by the heart
Defined by the sunrise and sunsets of your soul.

Baggage Claim

There was a knuckle knock in my heart, ignored one too many times
Resisted letting you in, fearful of rejection for I was broken
Love has been unkind, unable to compartmentalize the heartbreaks in my life
Carrying a backpack of emotional baggage, full of pain, and misery.

Everything happens for a reason, nothing is permanent
Romanticize the moment, heartbreak is a temporary discomfort
Love is not neatly packaged with a bow, it unravels and causes a mess
Be empathetic to life's meltdowns, learn to throw caution to the wind.

Energy drained, burdened with a heavy load of heart ache, filled to capacity
Need to unpack the weight of the past, and reclaim the present
Occupy the heart with a fresh start, seek therapy for healing suits all cases
Rediscover love once more for I am not a fraud, just a hopeless romantic trying to survive.

Your heart became my compass, strapped with a second chance
Clutched together to unpack the heartburn of hurt, sorrow, and doubt
Reload the trunk with new memories, hallmark moments, and true love
Content creator of my life, changed my circumstance, in an alliance with romance.

No longer bursting at the seams, sewn into your heart
Stepped up, made a move, in love with all that our relationship encompasses
Loving life, embracing my heart, opening the door to my future
Thought it was impossible, surpassed my expectations, my love is you.

Chocolate Sunshine

Impossible not to crave you when I lay alone
Promising to love you when I no longer see you
Listening in silence when I no longer hear your voice
Cradling the pillow when I no longer smell your scent.
Restless upon sliding my hand to an empty side of the bed
Clutching the sheets, thinking of our last night of intimacy
Moonlight glow energized our bodies, skins perspired in sweat
Choke hold by your warm caress, feeling the muscling between my legs.
Panted feverishly until your chocolate sunshine oozed thru my body
Ushered by tender kisses, souls surrendering to passion
The apex of our love continued, a comradery of our unending devotion
Spooned tightly, exhausted, mated souls immortally connected.
Sleeping alone is underrated, I miss your strokes of affection
Reluctant to interrupt my thoughts, unwilling to just see you in my dreams
Painful yearns, deep dejection, countless lonely nights
Involuntary accepting that your love no longer resides with mines.
Unbeknownst to you, our last tryst created an unsolicited gift
A ray of sunshine to clouded days, a blessing or maybe even a curse
Whichever way our love blows, time will be patient
Pleased to host your child in my womb, resuscitating the love of one's life.

harmon*I*o*U*s

Saddened to admit that love has eluded my grasp on many occasions
Caught in the middle of heartbreak, breakdown, and heartache
Journeyed from a place that dwelled in hurt and disappointment
Burn down chart of emotional deficit, but learned to survive through it all.

Honored in disbelief that you've asked me to be your future
Requested to be the owner of my heart, sole possessor of my soul
In cahoots to quench the thirst of romance, and swill the overflow of passion
Retribution on cupid absolved, ready to detangle the web of broken promises.

Touched me through the pain, changed the flesh of my heart
Strength in the number of two, memorializing the union of one
Tying the knot, committing to love every crawl space of our being
Drunk in the happy water of our love, sober-minded in happiness and faith.

Out of hiatus, you came to be the one for me, forbidden to leave
Made for right now, this moment, your life in mines
Reading between the lines, speaking to my body in tongues
Feeling good inside my love, no longer foreign to my spirit, amalgamated.

Follow the passion, love without tripping over prickled heartstrings
Rebuke the anguish of a lonely heart, accompany the rhythm of your aura
Divorce the pain, marry selflessly at the altar, vow to one another
Spouse nuptials, integrate last name, and wedlock in mind, body, and soul.

Happy Heart

A new love has rooted itself in my heart, implanted seeds of happiness
Introduced laughter in my eyes, warmth in my touch, and bliss to my spirit
Candlelight mood, floating bubbles of sunbeams, no more tears of a clown.

Heart fluttering, rushing to greet you, and dote on your love
Amorous advances accepted, idolizing each other from first light to midnight
Privileged to seduce these outstretch of emotions, powerless to contain the excitement.

Anytime, anyplace, joy hustling to host our desires, and emcee our bodies
Heavy breathing of careless whispers, begging time not to rush away
Making up the rules and breaking them along the way, surrendering to all temptations.

Stroked my heartstrings until unraveled, embroidered a passcode under my breast
Souls locked, rhythm intertwined, sole keeper of my throbbing wind chime
Caught up in your love, music to my ears, and chorister to our romantic playlist.

Love surfing the waves of the rainbow, admiring the colors of our aura
Favorite part of you is me, promising to be the forever crayon in your life
Painted caricatures, dancing in the exhibition of our everlasting anime.

You are the man of my dreams, stargazer in my orbit, twin to my silhouette
Because of you, I chose not to choose anyone else, victor to my love
Never have to be alone, my umbrella against all odds, until death do us part.

Life's Dust Devil

Mentally burnt out by life's standstill
Awaiting on past-due responses
Endlessly saving for an unaffordable overdue vacation
Willing to accept the unknown without caring for its ramifications.
Feeling fundamentally incompatible with life's offering
Attempting to take matters into your own hands
Resolutely trying to uncuff the dead weight
An invisible anvil anchored to suppress any glimpse of aspirations.
Doubtfully questioning life's reasons and blessings
Allowing grappling naysayers to place obstacles on every turn
Interrupting the ebb and flow of your existence
Determined to keep you stuck in reverse with no options.

Underrated, for no one dictates my life's seasons
The fight in me has no expiration date
Bygone to the bystander of letting others steal my joy
Walking away in my own power, trailblazer to future destinations.
Moving forward with turbulent anxieties
Allegiance to no one, policing the surrounded feculence
Freeing the mind and soul of negative pollution
One woman's monopoly, winning in the game of life's expectations.

About the Author

Milagros Diaz was born in the beautiful rich island of Puerto Rico but mainly raised in the New England tristate area. Although she moved around growing up, she always found time to write since her high school years. Writing engrosses her; she loves love. It absorbs her. Love fascinates her—the depth, the width—just the different feelings and emotions it encompasses. We all go through life and the waves it creates; Milagros puts these words into motion in her letters and writings on a page.

    When Milagros is not writing, she's busy salsa dancing, cooking a new recipe with a dollop of love, spending time with her family and friends, working, or watching the Hallmark channel. Her life is in the words of this book. Milagros is always inspired in the little nothings of life no matter what she's doing—feeding her cat, chatting with family, loving her children, spending time full of belly laughs with friends, and even pillow talking with a significant other. Her words are powerful.

She leads with love; her heart is in everything she does. As her thoughts take form, she jots it down anywhere and with anything. Words and phrases take shape on the bathroom mirror with lipstick, on toilet paper with a Sharpie, sticky notes on the wall, computer, and bedside table or just pulled over on the side of the road and text it to herself. Love motivates Milagros in her writings and in her life.

She is a friend, a mother, a sister, and a significant part of people's lives—she is love. She believes love is the one thing that makes the world go round. Love is conceived, birthed, and matured within our life experiences in its purest form. The words in this book are her expression of love. She once read on a blog: "El amor siempre está presente, no pasa de moda y es que es una experiencia a la que no debemos renunciar aunque hayamos sufrido alguna decepción previa." This quote is the way Milagros feels about love. Love shapes our being and soothes our soul. Milagros simply loves being in love with love.

www.ingramcontent.com/pod-product-compliance
Lightning Source LLC
Chambersburg PA
CBHW041952180426
43199CB00038B/2891